ORIGAMI
SUNCATCHERS

20 Dazzling Stars for Your Windows

Christine Gross-Loh

STERLING INNOVATION
New York

STERLING INNOVATION
New York

An Imprint of Sterling Publishing
387 Park Avenue South
New York, NY 10016

Package and book design by Melissa Gerber
All room photography © iStockphoto.com except:
Pg 15: © Dana Hoff/Beateworks/Corbis
Pg 19: © Image Source/Corbis
Pg 23: © Kate Kunz/Corbis
Pg 27: © Dana Hoff/Beateworks/Corbis
Project photos © Christopher C. Bain
Step-by-step photos © Leonard Hospidor

The suncatcher templates in this book were developed by Christine Gross-Loh, with the exception of the
traditional eight-point star, tulip, and medal, which were traditional designs.

ISBN 978-1-4351-26893

This book is part of the *Origami Suncatchers* kit and is not to be sold separately.

Distributed in Canada by Sterling Publishing
c/o Canadian Manda Group, 165 Dufferin Street
Toronto, Ontario, Canada M6K 3H6
Distributed in the United Kingdom by GMC Distribution Services
Castle Place, 166 High Street, Lewes, East Sussex, England BN7 1XU
Distributed in Australia by Capricorn Link (Australia) Pty. Ltd.
P.O. Box 704, Windsor, NSW 2756, Australia

For information about custom editions, special sales, and premium and corporate purchases,
please contact Sterling Special Sales at 800-805-5489 or specialsales@sterlingpublishing.com.

Manufactured in China

2 4 6 8 10 9 7 5 3

www.sterlingpublishing.com

CONTENTS

INTRODUCTION

Origami is the art of paper folding, which originated in Japan. The beauty of this craft lies in the enchanting fact that a few simple geometric folds can turn a plain piece of paper into something magical. Origami is soothing and meditative as far as papercrafts go, and it yields quick yet pleasing results.

Combine the basic geometric principles of origami with translucent, jewel-toned paper like what's included in this kit and you will create stunning suncatchers. Hang a few of them in a window and they will brighten your home instantly when sunlight filters through the transparent layers.

Making star-shaped origami suncatchers involves using eight, ten, or sixteen square or rectangular pieces of paper in colors of your choice. Sometimes a combination of two different colors, or even a different color for each single point of your star, are lovely, while other times the beauty of intricate folds is accentuated when you make your suncatcher all one color. Different color choices can create dramatically different results, even when using the same star pattern.

For each suncatcher you will fold each of the eight, ten, or sixteen pieces of paper the same way and then glue them together, slightly overlapping, to form a circular pattern. Make a variety in different colors and change them with the seasons—a rainbow-colored star brightens up a window looking out onto a snowy winter landscape, whereas a gorgeous yellow and orange sun-shaped one is spectacular in summer.

The suncatchers in this kit are arranged in order from simple to more complex. At the end are a few traditional origami patterns that you can make to create flowers and other shapes to hang in your window.

As you get accustomed to the way that certain folds create patterns in the end results, you will find yourself experimenting with folds of your own, and I highly encourage you to do this.

GET STARTED

R eady to begin? Start by taking a good look at the windows in your home and think about what kind of origami suncatcher you want to make and what colors appeal to you. You could begin with a small accent piece or go bold with a large, vibrant star. As you work on different designs you'll find that each has its own unique character. I generally like to take a look at the room itself as well as the scenery outside the window for inspiration and ideas. There is plenty of paper provided in this kit for you to experiment with both color and style, so go ahead and let your creativity loose.

Tools and Materials

Making origami suncatchers is very simple. No complicated material is required. All you need, besides the paper and glue stick provided in this kit, are a pair of sharp scissors and a bit of double-sided adhesive tape to attach the suncatchers to your windows.

Tips and Techniques

To begin most of the projects in this book, you will need to cut your paper to the appropriate size. To do this, fold each piece of paper into fourths (a horizontal, then a vertical fold) and then unfold and cut carefully along the lines so that you get four equal small square pieces of paper.

Origami requires very precise folds and a smidgen of patience. Most of the stars in this book begin with a vertical fold down the middle of each point. When doing this and all other folds, fold carefully, making sure your edges are lined up and even. Complete and then glue down the folds for each point first, and then assemble your suncatcher by gluing the points together as directed.

Dab lightly on the inner corners or inner edges of your folds to glue them down, and then press down briefly to secure. Use a light touch when gluing—you don't need a lot of pressure.

It can be helpful to have a small, slightly damp rag nearby to wipe your fingers when using the glue stick, but be sure your fingers are completely dry when handling the paper to prevent crinkling.

When assembling, be sure to line your points up precisely and check to see that the sides and corners meet where they should, as indicated in the instructions.

THE PROJECTS

Simple Eight-Point Star

Minimum folding makes this classic star deceptively simple yet stunning, especially if you cluster a few stars made of contrasting colors together on a window. By making this star in a single color, you're able to appreciate the beauty of the same color in single, double, triple, and even quadruple layers. As the layers increase, the colors deepen and take on the appearance of a multifaceted jewel.

a. Cut two pieces of paper into four squares each as detailed in the Tips and Techniques section on page 10. You'll create eight small squares. Each will become one point of the star.

b. To fold each point, place a square in front of you on the diagonal as shown. Fold it in half from side to side. Press hard on the crease and then unfold.

c. Now fold the upper sides down toward the center so that they meet along the center crease, as shown.

Glue the folds and press them down. Repeat steps b and c until you have eight points.

d. Once you have folded all eight points, begin assembling the star as shown: Place one point down in front of you with the folded side up. Swipe the glue stick on the lower right triangle section. Then place a second point on top as shown, with the bottom corners touching. These corners will form the very center of the star. The second point should partly overlap the first, so that its left lower edge lines up with the first point's center crease.

e. Keep adding more points.

f. Continue in this way around the circle until you have one point left. There should be just enough room for you to insert this point in place and complete the circle. The last point is placed on top of the point before it and underneath the first point of the circle, and glued, thus completing the pattern. This secures all the points together and makes your star complete.

g. The completed suncatcher.

Rainbow Star

This is a variation on the basic eight-point star that demonstrates the versatility of rainbow colors.

Cut one small square (a quarter of a sheet of paper) of each of the following colors: yellow, pink, orange, red, purple, blue, dark green, and light green. Each will become one point of the star.

a. To fold each point, place a square in front of you on the diagonal as shown. Fold it in half from side to side. Press hard on the crease and then unfold.

b. Now fold the upper sides down toward the center so that they meet along the center crease, as shown. Glue the folds and press them down. Repeat steps a and b until you have eight points.

c. Once you have folded all eight points, begin assembling the star as shown, keeping the colors in the order indicated above—yellow, pink, orange, red, purple, blue, dark green, and light green. Place one point down in front of you with the folded side up. Swipe the glue stick on the lower right triangle

section. Then place a second point on top as shown, with bottom corners touching. These corners will form the very center of the star. The second point should partly overlap the first, so that its left lower edge lines up with the first point's center crease.

d. Keep adding more points.

e. Continue in this way around the circle until you have one point left. There should be just enough room for you to insert this point in place and complete the circle. Lastly, glue the first point over the last point. This secures all the points together and makes your star complete.

f. The completed suncatcher.

Curvy Star

Origami sometimes creates unexpected curves where you would expect to see straight lines. This star is an example of the organic allure of soft curved lines. This makes a lovely filter for the sunlight streaming through your window.

Using one piece of paper in the color of your choice, cut it into eighths as shown in the Tips and Techniques section on page 10.

a. To create each point, place one rectangle in front of you as shown.

b. Fold the rectangle in half lengthwise to make a crease and then unfold.

c. Fold all four corners toward the center so they meet along the center crease.

d. Fold the upper two sides down toward the center one more time so they meet along the crease again. Glue down all corners and folds to secure. Repeat steps a–d until you have eight points.

e. Once you have folded all eight points, begin assembling the star. Place one point down in front of you with the folded side up. Swipe the glue stick on the lower right triangle section. Then place a second point on top, with bottom corners touching. These corners will form the very center of the star. The second point should partly overlap the first, so that its left lower edge lines up with the first point's center crease.

f. Keep adding more points. Continue in this way around the circle until you have one point left. There should be just enough room for you to insert this point in place and complete the circle. Lastly, glue the first point over the last point. This secures all the points together and makes your star complete.

g. The completed suncatcher.

Two-Color Curvy Star

This star is constructed just like the previous project, Curvy Star, but you will use two different colors to create contrast and a strikingly different look. Assemble with alternating colors, keeping in mind the way the colors will appear when they overlap.

Some combinations to try are blue and green, pink and yellow, yellow and orange, pink and blue, pink and orange, or pink and green.

Pick two colors and cut one piece of paper in each color into eighths, as detailed in the Tips and Techniques section on page 10. You'll use four rectangles of each color.

a. To create each point, place one rectangle in front of you as shown.

b. Fold the rectangle in half lengthwise to make a crease and then unfold.

c. Fold all four corners down toward the center so they meet along the center crease.

d. Fold the upper two sides down toward the center one more time so they meet along the crease again. Glue down all corners and folds to secure. Repeat steps a–d until you have eight points.

e. Once you have folded all eight points, begin assembling the star, alternating colors. Place one point down in front of you with the folded side up. Swipe the glue stick on the lower right triangle section. Then place a second point, on top of the alternate color, with bottom corners touching. These corners will form the very center of the star. The second point should partly overlap the first, so that its left lower edge lines up with the first point's center crease.

f. Keep adding more points. Continue in this way around the circle until you have one point left. There should be just enough room for you to insert this point in place and complete the circle. Lastly, glue the first point over the last point. This secures all the points together and makes your star complete.

g. The completed suncatcher.

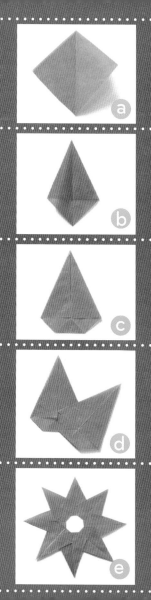

Open-Center Star

Here is a version of the Simple Eight-Point Star with a fun twist: an open space at the center.

Cut two pieces of paper into fourths so that you have eight squares.

a. To make each point, hold a square on the diagonal as shown, fold it from side to side, and then unfold to make a center crease.

b. Fold the upper two sides down toward the center to meet along the crease.

c. Fold the bottom triangle tip up until it just meets the other two corners, as shown, and glue all folds in place. Continue steps a–c until you have completed all eight points.

d. Assemble by aligning the bottom left diagonal edge of the first point with the center crease of the second point, as shown.

e. Like with the previous suncatcher projects, continue gluing points around the circle until you have one left. The last point is placed on top of half of the point before it, and underneath half of the first point of the circle, thus completing the pattern.

Open-Center Curvy Star

The combination of curvy lines and an open center make this a particularly tranquil suncatcher to gaze upon. The folds are not complicated but when placed together, all of the translucent layers form a satisfyingly rich pattern.

Cut two pieces of paper into fourths so that you have eight squares.

a. Holding each square at a diagonal, fold it from side to side and then unfold to make a center crease.

b. Fold two side corners so that they meet at the middle crease and glue in place.

c. Fold the upper two sides down toward the center so they meet along the center crease. Glue in place.

d. Fold the bottom corner up so that it fits into the triangle created by the folds from Step c, and then unfold to make a light crease. Don't press too hard to make this crease, as it will be visible later on.

e. Fold the bottom corner upwards so that it meets the crease created in Step d. Press, and glue in place. Repeat steps a–e until you have eight points.

f. Assemble by aligning the bottom left slanted side of one point with the center crease of another point, as shown. Make sure that the bottom corner of the slanted side of the first point is lined up with the bottom of the second point.

Continue in this way around the circle until you have one point left. There should be just enough room for you to insert this point in place and complete the circle. Lastly, glue the first point over the last point (as shown in previous suncatcher projects—see Simple Eight-Point Star on page 14, steps d–f). This secures all the points together and makes your star complete.

g. The completed suncatcher.

Square Star

The combination of clean geometric lines and multifaceted layers make this suncatcher appealing no matter which color you use. Try making this star in several different colors and hang them as a bright and cheerful cluster.

Cut two pieces of paper into fourths so that you have eight squares.

a. Fold each square from side to side so that you create a crease going through the middle, as shown.

b. Fold the upper corners in and down toward the center crease and then unfold to create two new creases.

c. Fold the upper corners again, this time only toward the new creases made in Step b. Fold over one more time as shown.

d. Glue the folds down.

Fold the bottom corners all the way to the center crease and glue down. Continue steps a–d until you have eight points.

e. Assemble your star by aligning the lower left side of one point on the center crease of another point, with bottom corners touching. These corners will form the very center of the star.

f. Continue in this way around the circle until you have one point left. There should be just enough room for you to insert this point in place and complete the circle. Finally, glue the first point over the last point as shown in previous suncatcher examples. (See Simple Eight-Point Star on page 14, steps d–f.) This secures all the points together.

g. The completed suncatcher.

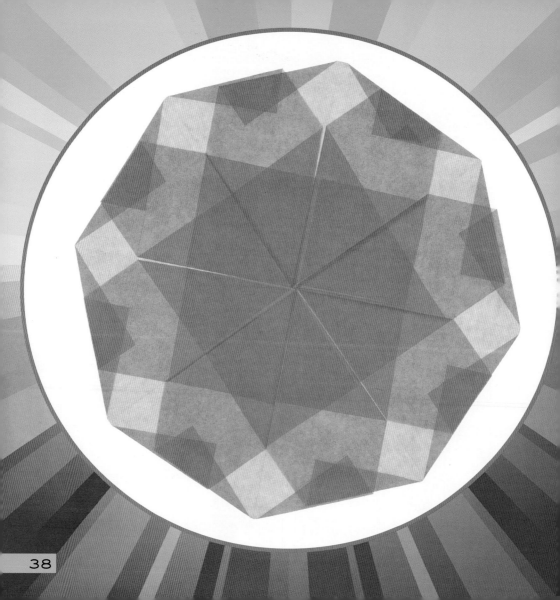

Round Star

This spectacular suncatcher is best done in one color because the pieces overlap each other almost completely. It's best highlighted by using a bright color like yellow or orange. An ethereal flower floats in the middle, framed by different shades of color on the edges.

Cut two pieces of paper into fourths, so that you have eight squares.

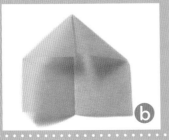

a. To make each point, take a piece of paper and fold it down the middle from side to side as shown and then unfold to reveal a crease down the middle.

b. Fold the top corners in and down so that they meet at the center crease and then unfold.

c. Fold the top corners down so that the upper sides line up with the creases formed in Step b. Glue in place.

d. Fold the lower two corners up so that the bottom sides meet along the center crease. Repeat steps a–d until you have eight points.

e. Assemble your star by aligning the lower left side of one point on the center crease of a second point, with bottom corners touching. These corners will form the very center of the star.

Continue in this way around the circle until you have one point left. There should be just enough room for you to insert this point in place and complete the circle. Lastly, glue the first point over the last point as shown in previous suncatcher examples. (See Simple Eight-Point Star on page 14, steps d–f.) This secures all the points together and makes your star complete.

f. The completed suncatcher.

Blue Flower Star

This design relies on the use of eight rectangular pieces of paper to create a delicate suncatcher that resembles a starflower. This suncatcher is especially pretty when created in blue or other jewel tones.

a. Cut one piece of blue paper into eighths as shown in the Tips and Techniques section on page 10, so that you have eight rectangles.

b. Fold each rectangle in half lengthwise and then unfold to create a center crease, as shown.

c. Next, fold each side in toward the center crease. Press and then unfold to create two more lengthwise creases.

d. Fold each side edge inward toward the nearest crease—the creases created in Step c—and press hard. The paper will stay folded once you make several other folds, so you don't need to glue them down.

e. Fold each top corner in and down to meet at the center crease.

f. Fold each upper side in toward the center one more time to meet along the center crease. Press and glue down.

g. Fold each bottom corner up to meet along the center crease. Press and glue down. Repeat steps a–g until you have eight points.

h. Assemble your star by aligning the lower left side of one point on the center crease of a second point, with bottom corners touching. These corners will form the very center of the star.

Continue in this way around the circle until you have one point left. There should be just enough room for you to insert this point in place and complete the circle. Finally, glue the first point over the last point as shown in previous suncatcher examples. (See Simple Eight-Point Star on page 14, steps d–f.) This secures all the points together.

i. The completed suncatcher.

Red Rose Star

Chunky petals and simple lines make a sweet, basic star that is so easy, even children can make it. Making this in a single bold color, such as red, highlights the complicated patterns that emerge when fitting the points together. This makes a delightful accent for a small window, or you can make two in one color and two in a contrasting color and alternate them to liven up a larger space.

Take one piece of paper and cut it into eighths so that you have eight rectangles. Each will become one point of the star.

a. To make each point, take a piece of paper and fold it in half lengthwise, press, and then unfold.

Fold the top corners in and down so that the upper sides meet along the center crease. Glue down.

b. Fold the bottom corners up so that the lower sides meet along the center crease. Glue down. Repeat steps a and b until you have eight points.

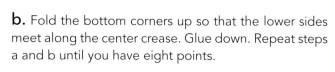

c. Assemble your star by aligning the lower left side of one point on the center crease of a second point, with bottom corners touching. These corners will form the very center of the star.

Continue in this way around the circle until you have one point left. There should be just enough room for you to insert this point in place and complete the circle. Lastly, glue the first point over the last point as shown in previous suncatcher examples. (See Simple Eight-Point Star on page 14, steps d–f.) This secures all the points together.

d. The completed suncatcher.

Pinwheel Star

This suncatcher has slightly asymmetrical points. When it's assembled, it looks somewhat like a pinwheel. It's best displayed when done all in one rich color, such as blue or green. This is very simple to create, but looks impressively complicated.

Cut two pieces of paper into fourths so that you have eight squares.

a. Holding each square at a diagonal, fold it from side to side and then unfold to make a center crease.

b. Fold the two side triangle tips toward the middle crease and glue in place.

c. Fold the upper two sides in and down toward the center so they meet along the center crease. Glue in place.

d. Next, take the lower right edge of the point and fold it so that it lies along the center crease. Glue in place. Repeat steps a–d until you have completed all eight points.

e. Assemble your star by aligning the lower left side of one point on the center crease of a second point, with bottom corners touching. These corners will form the very center of the star.

Continue in this way around the circle until you have one point left. There should be just enough room for you to insert this point in place and complete the circle. Lastly, glue the first point over the last point as shown in previous suncatcher examples. (See Simple Eight-Point Star on page 14, steps d–f.) This secures all the points together.

f. The completed suncatcher.

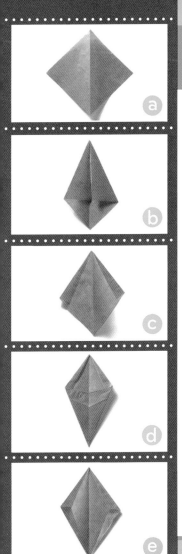

Ten-Point Star

This is a very pretty star when done in a pale pastel such as yellow, pink, or orange. Ten points don't fit together as easily as eight or sixteen, so this is the only suncatcher in this kit where you will want to place your points together before actually securing them with glue.

Take three pieces of paper in the same color and cut into fourths. You will use ten of these squares.

a. Hold a square on the diagonal, as shown, and fold from side to side and then unfold.

b. Fold the upper sides in and down to meet along the center crease. Press as lightly as possible and unfold.

c. Now fold the upper sides in toward the creases you just created in Step b. Press and glue in place.

d. Fold the bottom sides up to meet at the center crease. Press as lightly as possible and then unfold.

e. Fold the bottom sides up to meet the creases you just created in Step d. Press and glue in place. Repeat steps a–e until you have completed ten points.

f. To assemble this star, it's best to place the points in position before actually gluing them down. Make a loop of cellophane tape, sticky side out, and place it on your work surface. Assemble your star on top of the loop of tape at the center. It will lightly hold pieces in place but is easy to remove when you've completed your suncatcher. Place the lower left side of the first point so that it is just about a millimeter or two off of the center crease of the second point, with bottom corners touching. These corners will form the very center of the star.

g. Continue in this way around the circle until you have one point left. There should be just enough room for you to insert this point in place and complete the circle.

h. Take a last look to make sure that the points are evenly spaced. Finally, glue all points in place.

i. The completed suncatcher.

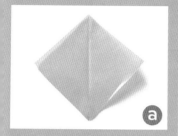

This is a gorgeous star—absolutely breathtaking in a window at the height of summer.

Take four pieces of paper in the same color and cut each into fourths so that you have sixteen squares.

a. To make each point, fold a square in half along the diagonal, press, and unfold to create a center crease.

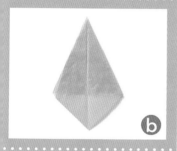

b. Fold the upper edges in and down toward the center, so that they lie along the center crease.

c. Fold the lower edges up toward the center so that they lie along the center crease. Press and glue down. Repeat steps a–c until you have sixteen points.

Sixteen-Point Multicolor Star

This suncatcher is sure to attract lots of compliments. It can be made all in one color, but using four different colors distributed throughout makes for a unique and eye-catching decoration. The star shown here uses orange, pink, yellow, and green. If you try your own color combination, light pastels combine nicely together and seem to work better than jewel tones.

Cut four pieces of paper in orange, pink, yellow, and green (or colors of your choosing) into fourths so that you have sixteen squares.

a. Holding each square at a diagonal, fold it from side to side and then unfold to make a center crease.

b. Fold both side triangle tips in toward the middle crease and glue in place.

c. Fold the upper two sides in and down toward the center so they meet along the center crease. Glue in place.

d. Fold the bottom two sides up toward the center so they meet along the center crease. Glue in place. Repeat steps a–d until you have four points in four colors—sixteen in all.

e. Assemble your star by aligning the lower left side of one point on the center crease of a second point, with bottom corners touching. These corners will form the very center of the star. Place colors in this order around the star: orange, pink, yellow, green, then back to pink and so forth.

Continue in this way around the circle until you have one point left. There should be just enough room for you to insert this point in place and complete the circle. Lastly, glue the first point over the last point as shown in previous suncatcher projects. (See Simple Eight-Point Star on page 14, steps d–f.) This secures all the points together.

f. The completed suncatcher.

Sixteen-Point Crimson Star

This is a beautifully vivid star when done in a bold jewel tone, such as red.

Take four sheets of red paper and cut each into fourths so that you have sixteen squares.

a. To make each point, take a square and hold it at a diagonal, then fold from side to side. Press to make a center crease and then unfold.

b. Fold the lower sides up toward the center so that they meet along the center crease.

c. Fold the upper sides in and down toward the center so that they meet along the center crease. Glue in place.

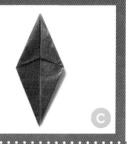

d. Fold the upper sides in about a fraction of an inch, as shown, and press well. Glue in place. (You don't have to measure; eyeballing this fold should be adequate.) Repeat steps a–d until you have completed all sixteen points.

e. Assemble your star by aligning the lower left side of one point on the center crease of a second point, with bottom corners touching. These corners will form the very center of the star.

Continue in this way around the circle until you have one point left. There should be just enough room for you to insert this point in place and complete the circle. Last, glue the first point over the last point as shown in previous suncatcher projects. (See Simple Eight-Point Star on page 14, steps d–f.) This secures all the points together.

f. The completed suncatcher.

74

Sixteen-Point Green Star

Green is serene. Any room with this lovely green suncatcher in its window will instantly feel tranquil and calm.

Take four sheets of green paper and cut each into fourths so that you have sixteen squares.

a. To make each point, take a square and hold it at a diagonal, then fold from side to side. Press to make a center crease and then unfold.

b. Fold the two side triangle tips toward the middle crease and glue in place.

c. Fold the upper two sides in and down toward the center so they meet along the center crease. Glue in place.

d. Fold the upper two sides inward and down one more time a fraction of an inch and press down well.

e. Fold the bottom two sides up toward the center so that they meet along the center crease. Press well and glue in place. These should be glued down securely so that these folds anchor the upper folds in place. Repeat steps a–e until you have sixteen points.

f. Assemble your star by aligning the lower left side of one point on the center crease of a second point, with bottom corners touching. These corners will form the very center of the star.

Continue in this way around the circle until you have one point left. There should be just enough room for you to insert this point in place and complete the circle. Last, glue the first point over the last point as shown in previous suncatcher projects. (See Simple Eight-Point Star on page 14, steps d–f.) This secures all the points together.

g. The completed suncatcher.

Tulip Suncatcher

This pretty little flower is one of the first projects Japanese children make when learning origami. The flower itself is very simple and the stem is not much harder. Make a whole garden of these to enhance your windows in spring.

Cut a pink piece of paper into four squares. You'll use one of those squares to make the tulip.

a. Turn the square on the diagonal.

b. Fold the square in half to make a triangle.

c. Fold the sides of the triangle from the center so that they peek out like tulip petals, as shown. Glue them in place and turn the flower over.

To make the stem, take a piece of green paper and cut into four squares. You'll use one of these to make a stem and a leaf.

d. Hold the square on a diagonal and fold it in thirds, as shown.

e. Fold the triangle in half lengthwise.

f. To make a leaf, fold the bottom at an angle upward (about one-third of the way from the bottom).

g. Glue to the pink flower to complete the tulip suncatcher.

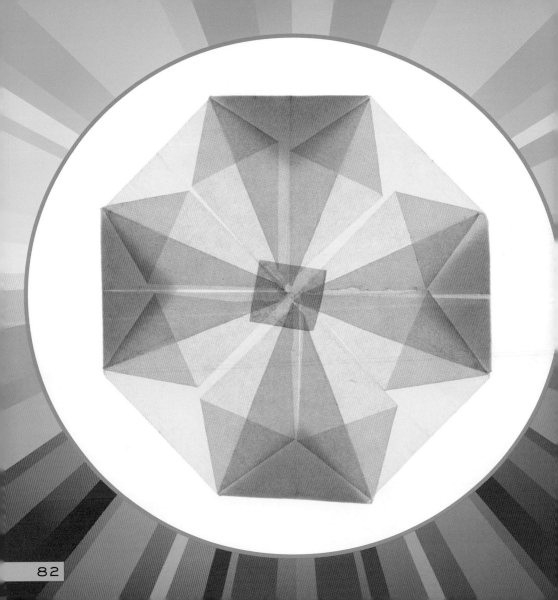

This is an example of classic origami. When made with regular origami paper, it's used as a medal or brooch. Created with the transparent paper contained in this kit, it appears completely different because of the way the light shines through the layers, and makes a sweet decorative ornament for a small window.

Take one piece of paper. Do not cut.

a. Fold it in half from top to bottom and then unfold to create a center crease.

b. Next, fold the upper and lower edges to meet at the center crease. Press down.

c. Fold from side to side, press, and then unfold to create a center crease.

d. Fold the two side edges toward the center so that they meet along the center crease. Press.

e. Rotate one-quarter turn clockwise. Insert your finger into the corner inside each open flap and pull out a triangle as shown. Press. Repeat this for all four corners.

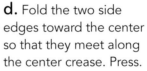

f. Next, push each pulled out corner back in as shown (this is called the Squash Fold).

g. Fold the edges of each of those four corner square panels in toward the center crease of each corner square, as shown. You'll do this eight times in all—two for each corner square.

h. Insert your finger inside each of the folds you just made and then press the corners open, as shown. Repeat for all eight folds. Glue down folds if desired for a neater appearance.

i. Fold all four corners back as shown and secure in place with glue.

j. Finish off by cutting and gluing a small square or circle or other small shape in the very center.

Kirigami Star

This is similar to the Simple Eight-Point Star, except that you create a drastically new look in the final product by using scissors to make a simple cut-out design. This technique is called "kirigami," or the art of cutting folded paper. While origami is the art of folding paper (*oru*, in Japanese, means "fold," and *kami*—which turns into -*gami* whenever it's part of a compound word—means "paper"), the mere addition of one more step turns this into *kirigami*. *Kiru* means cut and *kami*, again, means paper. It's a quick way to create a distinctive-looking suncatcher.

Cut two pieces of paper into four equal-sized squares. You'll have eight small squares. Each will become one point of the star.

a. To fold each point, place a square in front of you on a diagonal as shown. Fold it in half from side to side. Press hard on the crease and then unfold.

b. Now fold the upper sides in and down toward the center so that they meet along the center crease, as shown. Dab your glue stick on the inner corners of those folds and then press down to lightly secure them in place. Repeat steps a and b until you have eight points.

c. Next, fold each point in half along the center crease and trim the tip of each point as shown, to create a rounded edge. To make sure the tips all match, either hold two or three points together at a time to cut, or else cut one point first and match that to the others when trimming them.

d. Cut a small triangle on the folded edge of one of the points halfway between the center and top. Repeat for all eight points, making sure to line them up with your first cut point so that they match. Glue down cut edges at the top of the point for a neat appearance.

e. Once you have folded and cut all eight points, begin assembling the star. Place one point down in front of you with the folded side up, swipe the glue stick on the lower right-hand section and then place a second point on top as shown, with bottom corners touching. These corners will form the very center of the star.

Continue in this way around the circle until you have one point left. There should be just enough room for you to insert this point in place and complete the circle. Last, glue the first point over the last point. This secures all the points together.

f. The completed suncatcher.

RESOURCES

Books

Magical Window Stars by Frederique Gueret (Floris Books)

Window Stars: Making Folded Stars from Colored Papers by Thomas Berger (HeartSong)

General Craft Supplies

A.C. Moore Arts & Crafts
www.acmoore.com

Hobby Lobby
www.hobbylobby.com

Jo-Ann Fabric and Craft Stores
www.joann.com

Michaels
www.michaels.com

Translucent Kite Paper

A Toy Garden
www.atoygarden.com

Nova Naturals
www.novanaturals.com

ABOUT THE AUTHOR

Christine Gross-Loh is a crafter and writer. She has four young children who inspire her every day. Visit her online at www.origamimommy.org.

CREATE A GALAXY OF RADIANT STARS FOR YOUR WINDOWS!

The art of folding paper is a fun craft that's easy to learn and provides lovely results. *Origami Suncatchers* adds a new dimension to this traditional craft, using colorful waxed paper to create beautiful ornaments that come alive when sunlight shines through their transparent layers. Inside you'll find easy to follow instructions for making 20 stunning designs. For each project, you'll cut and fold several sheets of paper, and then glue them together, slightly overlapping, to form a variety of colorful pinwheels, simple and complex stars, and other designs. Mix and match different colors of paper for dramatically different effects—the possibilities are infinite! These dazzling ornaments are a snap to make and you'll find designs and color combinations to suit any décor and taste.

STERLING INNOVATION
New York

STECK-VAUGHN
NEW WAY
HEADS and TAILS

Jip!

Acknowledgments
Executive Editor   Stephanie Muller
Design Coordinator   D Childress
Design   Clive Sutherland
Illustrations   David Mostyn
Electronic Production   Rmedia

ISBN 0-8172-8332-3

1   2   3   4   5   6   7   8   9   LB   01   00   99   98